Ferdinand Magellan

and the First Voyage
Around the World

Explorers of New Worlds

Ferdinand Magellan

and the First Voyage
Around the World

Jim Gallagher

Chelsea House Publishers
Philadelphia

To LaNelle
Thanks for your love and support,
and for making the journey so much fun.

Prepared for Chelsea House Publishers by:
OTTN Publishing, Warminster, PA

CHELSEA HOUSE PUBLISHERS
Editor in Chief: Stephen Reginald
Managing Editor: James D. Gallagher
Production Manager: Pamela Loos
Art Director: Sara Davis
Director of Photography: Judy L. Hasday
Senior Production Editor: LeeAnne Gelletly
Series Designer: Keith Trego

First Printing
1 3 5 7 9 8 6 4 2

Library of Congress Cataloging-in-Publication Data

Gallagher, Jim, 1969–
  Ferdinand Magellan / by Jim Gallagher
p.   cm. – (Explorers of new worlds)
Includes bibliographical references (p. 62) and index.
Summary: Presents a biography of the daring Portuguese
sea captain who commanded the first expedition that
sailed around the world.
ISBN 0-7910-5508-6 (hc)
1. Magalhães, Fernão de, d. 1521 Juvenile literature. 2.
Explorers–Portugal Biography Juvenile literature.   3.
Voyages around the world Juvenile literature. [1. Magellan, Ferdinand, d. 1521 2. Explorers. 3. Voyages around
the world.] I. Title. II. Series.
G286.M2G35   1999
910'.92—de21
                                        99-35229
                                           CIP

Contents

pugna, mare de Magellani ⟨⟩ Prima ego

Around the
World

Explorers of New Worlds

This woodcut shows the Victoria *arriving in Spain after its three-year voyage around the world. The ship has two masts instead of the usual three (one was lost in a storm). The* Victoria *was the only one of Ferdinand Magellan's five ships to return safely.*

I

t was early fall in southern Spain. Men working in the village of Sanlúcar de Barrameda, on the Atlantic coast, were surprised to see a rickety ship sail past the port. The small, battered sailing vessel, called a **caravel**, moved slowly up the nearby Guadalquivir River. Two days later, on September 8, 1522, the caravel *Victoria* docked at the port of Seville, 75 miles upriver.

When the *Victoria* had left Seville over three years

earlier, it had been in fine shape. Now, one of her three masts was gone. The other masts creaked painfully as the wind filled the patched and worn sails. The ship's timbers were worm-eaten and heavy with barnacles. The *Victoria* was leaking so badly that her crew had to constantly pump out seawater.

Only 18 members of the *Victoria*'s 50-man crew survived the long journey. They were starving and many were sick with **scurvy**. This is a disease that caused the sailors' gums to become swollen and tender and caused extreme pain in the joints of their arms and legs. During the long trip, the *Victoria*'s food supply had rotted and the fresh water had become stagnant and foul. When the food was all gone, the sailors had been forced to catch and eat rats aboard the ship. They even ate sawdust, wood chips, and pieces of leather that had been wrapped around the masts.

Yet the *Victoria*'s arrival in Seville was considered a triumph. The men who had survived were hailed as heroes. They had become the first to sail completely around, or ***circumnavigate***, the earth.

Everyone wanted to hear the tough survivors tell about their bold adventures on the world's oceans. The ship's captain, Juan Sebastián de Elcano, was invited to the Spanish court. There, King Charles praised Elcano for his incredible voyage of discovery. The sailor was given a reward and allowed to create a **coat of arms**. The symbol designed for Elcano was a globe wrapped in a banner reading, in Latin, "Thou first circumnavigated me."

Through all this, the role of another heroic captain was almost forgotten. He was Ferdinand Magellan, a native of Portugal. King Charles had placed Magellan in charge of the *Victoria* and four other ships in 1519. Magellan was short, dark-haired, and stern. He was a skilled sailor and a tough commander. When others wanted to give up, Magellan pushed and prodded the sailors to continue. Without his determination, the voyage probably would have failed.

But Magellan had died during the last leg of the journey, and his contributions were ignored by the Spanish. Instead, they honored Elcano, their countryman. Magellan might have been forgotten if not for a *Victoria* survivor named Antonio Pigafetta. In 1524, two years after the *Victoria* returned, Pigafetta wrote a popular account of the voyage. Thanks to his book, many Europeans learned about Ferdinand Magellan's courageous exploits for the first time.

The Spice Trade

This detail from an old book shows spices being harvested. The word "spices" was used for hundreds of products from the Far East, such as sugar, perfume, coffee, and tea. However, the true spices—pepper, nutmeg, mace, cinnamon, and cloves—were the most valuable to Europeans in the 15th century.

2

erdinand Magellan is a French variation of the Portuguese name Fernão de Magalhães. That is the name Ruy and Alda Magalhães gave their third child when he was born, sometime around 1480.

Not much is known about Ferdinand Magellan's early life. His parents were members of the Portuguese **nobility** (the upper class of society), so Magellan had many privileges. He had an older sister named Isabel and a brother named Diogo. In a few years, Alda Magalhães would give birth to two more daughters. Ferdinand and his family lived in northern Portugal, either in the small town of Sabrosa or in nearby Minho.

Portugal is a small country on the Iberian Peninsula. (A *peninsula* is a land area that is surrounded on three sides by water.) It is located between Spain and the Atlantic Ocean. Portugal's daring sailors helped make it one of the richest and most powerful countries in Europe during Ferdinand Magellan's lifetime. They did this by developing a sea trade with the countries of Asia.

In the 13th century, a young man named Marco Polo spent 25 years traveling across China. He later wrote a book about the wonders that he had seen: gold, fine silks and fabrics, and *spices* that were unknown to Europeans. His book was very popular.

Marco Polo had traveled to China, India, and Mongolia in a *caravan* of camels. However, in the years after his death the trade routes became dangerous. European merchants had to pass through lands controlled by hostile Arabs and Turks.

Even without these dangers, traveling to China by land was difficult. Marco Polo's first journey from Venice across China had taken over three years.

Venice was the home of Marco Polo in the 13th century. When Magellan was growing up nearly 200 years later, the Italian city was at the center of the spice trade.

However, goods from the East were in great demand. The most valuable were the spices, because they were not available in Europe at the time. This word was used for hundreds of products, such as sugar, perfume, coffee, and tea. Because it was hard to get to Asia, spices were very expensive.

To avoid the dangerous land routes, Indian and Arab traders sailed with cargoes of spices through the Indian Ocean. The shipments were then transported across the region now known as the Middle East. Eventually, the spices of Asia came to ports in the eastern area of the Mediterranean Sea. From there, the goods were distributed all over Europe. Two cities in northeastern Italy, Venice and Genoa, controlled the eastern Mediterranean. As a result, they grew rich from the spice trade.

European rulers were jealous of the wealth of Venice and Genoa. They dreamed of finding a new way to reach the East Indies. By cutting out the Italian merchants and the Arab sailor-traders, they could make enormous profits.

In 1419, a Portuguese ruler named Prince Henry started his nation on a search for a sea route to the East Indies. Prince Henry, later known as the Navigator, was interested in *geography* (the study of the

Prince Henry the Navigator (1394–1460) is one of the most important figures of Portuguese history. The school of navigation that he founded and the missions of exploration that he encouraged helped Portugal become a rich and powerful nation in the 16th century.

earth) and exploration. Henry believed that it was possible to sail to Asia from Portugal. He founded a school to teach sailing and **navigation**. He also sent out expeditions seeking a sea passage to Asia. Portugal would become rich if it could find the way.

Gradually, Portuguese sailors traveled south along the edge of Africa, mapping the coastline. By the time Prince Henry the Navigator died in 1460, an expedition had rounded the westernmost point of the continent. The kings who followed Henry continued sending out ships. In 1473, a Portuguese ship crossed the **equator**. When Magellan was about eight years old, a Portuguese captain named Bartolomeu Dias rounded the southern tip of Africa and sailed into the Indian Ocean. Although Dias turned back before he reached the Indies, he had proved that Prince Henry had been right. It was possible to reach Asia by sailing east.

As Portuguese ships continued to map out the route to the Indies, Ferdinand Magellan grew to manhood. When he was about 12 years old, his parents sent him to Lisbon, the capital city of Portugal, where he would serve as an assistant (called a *page*) to the queen. This was a privilege, for it meant that he, like the other pages, would receive an education. They would be trained as future leaders of Portugal.

While at the royal court in Lisbon, Magellan's studies included geography, navigation, and *astronomy*. He also learned about the great Portuguese sailor-explorers, as well as an Italian named Christopher Columbus who had made a great discovery for Portugal's neighbor, Spain. In 1492, the year Magellan became a page, Columbus sailed west across the Atlantic Ocean and landed in what he believed were the East Indies. Despite this, the Portuguese kept seeking their own route to the east, around Africa.

When Magellan was 16, he was given the rank of

squire and a position as a clerk in the Casa da India. This was a government bureau that organized sailing expeditions. In 1497, he may have helped keep records and buy supplies for a trip led by Vasco da Gama. The four ships commanded by da Gama rounded the southern cape of Africa and sailed to India. Da Gama loaded his ship with spices and returned to Lisbon in 1499. At last, Portugal had its direct sea route to the Indies.

War in the
Indian
Ocean

In 1497, Vasco da Gama sailed around the Cape of Good Hope, a point near the southernmost tip of Africa, and reached the East Indies. This opened up a lucrative trade route that made Portugal very wealthy.

3

At the time Vasco da Gama reached the Indies, his voyage was far more important than Columbus's. The New World the Italian explorer had discovered had not yet proved valuable to Spain. Meanwhile, Portugal gained immediate benefits from its sea route. The small country quickly became rich as the center of the spice trade. Soon spices were selling in Lisbon for one-fifth the cost they had sold for a few years earlier.

However, the Arabs who controlled the Indian Ocean spice trade were unhappy. The Portuguese transported the goods themselves. This meant no profit for the Arabs. They declared war, attacking Portuguese ships as they traveled to the Indies.

In 1505, King Manoel of Portugal decided to fight back. He sent a fleet of 22 ships to destroy the Arab raiders. The expedition was commanded by Francisco de Almeida.

The war in the Indian Ocean was bloody and brutal. Because of differences in their religions, the Muslim Arabs and the Christian Portuguese hated each other. They rarely showed mercy when they met in battle.

Ferdinand Magellan was bored with his job at the Casa da India. He asked the king if he could join Portugal's navy. King Manoel gave the 25-year-old permission to enlist in Almeida's sailing force. Magellan and a close friend, Francisco Serrão, were assigned to a ship commanded by Francisco's older brother, João Serrão.

The ocean was rough as the fleet moved away from Portugal. After a long, stormy voyage, the ships rounded the Cape of Good Hope, a landmark near the southernmost tip of Africa. As the Portuguese *armada* sailed up the eastern coast of Africa, it stopped often to attack Arab trading posts.

Magellan was a good sailor. Soon he was promoted to pilot's assistant. This meant that he would help navigate his boat. Magellan was transferred to a new, flat-bottomed boat. This barge could be used only in the shallow waters close to the coast, but it was equipped with cannons to blow up Arab ships. Magellan quickly became expert in steering the small warship. In 15 months, he and his crew sank more than 200 Arab ships, called *dhows*.

In 1507, Magellan was reassigned to a regular sea vessel. For the next two years, he sailed the Indian Ocean with a captain named Nuno Pereira. They were involved in many minor battles with the Arabs. In one major encounter, they joined the entire Portuguese fleet, under the command of Francisco de Almeida, in wiping out the city of Dabul.

After this victory, Almeida took his 19 ships and about 1,800 men in a search for the Arab fleet. The Portuguese found their enemies–200 large dhows and about 20,000 men–at the island of Diu. Although his force seemed hopelessly outnumbered, Almeida ordered an attack. The Portuguese destroyed about half of the Arab naval force, but they suffered heavy casualties. Pereira was killed, and Magellan was badly wounded. Although he was not expected to survive, the scrappy sailor pulled through. Magellan spent the next five months in a hospital in Cochin, a trading post that had been captured by the Portuguese.

By September 1509, Magellan had rejoined the fleet. He was assigned to a group of five ships sailing to the important port of Malacca. The city, on the Malaysian Peninsula, was regularly visited by ships bearing goods from China, Arabia, India, Ceylon, and the Spice Islands. Almeida hoped to capture the coastal city from the natives, called Malays. This would give Portugal control over the Indian Ocean, and the spice trade, once and for all. The small fleet was commanded by Diogo Lopes de Sequeira. Magellan was pleased to find that his friend Francisco Serrão was also part of the expedition.

When the Portuguese reached Malacca, the **sultan** in charge of the city was not happy to see five heavily armed warships in his busy harbor. However, he had been warned about the damage Portuguese cannons could do. The sultan was friendly when he greeted the foreigners. He invited Sequeira's men to visit the city, and the captain gave

This image from an Arab manuscript shows the traditional sailing ship, or dhow, used on the Indian Ocean.

the sailors permission. Many sailors eagerly left the ships to explore life ashore. Sequeira invited one of the local leaders to his ship for a game of chess.

On the surface the situation appeared to be peaceful, but Magellan did not trust the sultan. He remained on his ship, even though most of the crew had gone ashore. When he noticed a large number of Malaysian canoes carrying men armed with knives approaching the ships, he warned Sequeira.

When the Malays attacked, sailors on the Portuguese ships were able to repel them. Those who had gone ashore were not so lucky. They were surprised by the native warriors and slaughtered. About 40 of the Portuguese, led by Francisco Serrão, managed to fight off the Malays and make their way onto a pier. Magellan bravely leapt into a small boat and rowed to the pier to save Serrão and several of the others. When they returned, Sequeira directed his ships safely out of Malacca harbor.

The expedition had been a disaster. About 60 men had been killed or captured. However, things might have been much worse if not for Magellan's vigilance and bravery. When Sequeira's fleet returned, Magellan was given command of his own ship. Francisco Serrão was also made a ship captain.

In 1510, Captain Magellan took part in a Portuguese attack on the port of Calicut. This turned into another disastrous defeat for the Portuguese, and Magellan was wounded in battle for the second time. Soon afterward, he decided to return home. As his reward for five years of hard fighting, he had accumulated a large amount of plundered spices. Magellan could sell this for a sizable fortune when he reached the capital of Portugal.

Unfortunately, Magellan was returning to Lisbon as a passenger aboard another captain's ship. This captain was not as good a sailor as Magellan. The ship hit a reef in the Indian Ocean. The passengers and crew escaped by swimming or rowing small boats to a nearby island.

Some of the officers and noblemen decided to row the small boats back to the nearest port, Cochin. They promised to send rescue ships to pick up the rest of the stranded men. Magellan agreed to stay behind with the ordinary sailors.

Magellan must have been nervous for the next three weeks. Although he had been promised that the rescue ships would be sent, he could not be certain that he would be rescued until he saw the masts of the vessel sent from Cochin. Magellan and the crew were saved, but the tough sailor had lost his chance to become rich. His spices had been ruined by the salt water.

Magellan was disappointed. It had taken him five years to accumulate his spice treasure, and a careless captain had wrecked his plans in a moment. Magellan decided to return to military service in the Indian Ocean and try again to gain riches.

In November 1510, he participated in one of the bloodiest battles of the war. Francisco de Almeida had been replaced as commander of Portugal's fleet by Afonso de Albuquerque. The new leader ordered an attack on Goa, a major trading city on the southern Malabar coast. Albuquerque gave Magellan command of a warship.

The Portuguese forces, directed by Albuquerque, overwhelmed the city. When Goa surrendered, Albuquerque brutally ordered that the city be entirely destroyed. In a single afternoon, more than 8,000 men, women, and children were killed by Albuquerque's men.

The destruction of Goa resulted in a great financial reward for almost every man who participated. Even the lowest-ranking soldiers received two years' pay as their share of the treasure. One man did not receive any reward for his part in the battle: Ferdinand Magellan. Many historians believe that the dark-haired captain was not rewarded because he refused to help slaughter the helpless citizens of Goa after the city surrendered.

Magellan remained one of Albuquerque's best captains, however. In July 1511 he directed one of 19 Portuguese ships in a second attempt on Malacca.

A small cannon still guards a gate in the fortified city of Malacca. Magellan's second attempt to take the Arab city was more successful than his first. In August 1511 Malacca surrendered to the Portuguese fleet.

This time, the city was bombarded with cannons until it surrendered on August 10, 1511. Magellan received a share in the plunder from the captured city, and he was appointed one of the military commanders of Malacca. He remained in the city until the end of the year, when he returned to Lisbon.

Ferdinand Magellan became obsessed with finding a passage through South America to the East Indies. He looked for clues in old maps, and asked experienced sailors for advice.

New Beginnings 4

When he arrived at the royal court in Lisbon in 1511, Magellan was in for an unpleasant surprise. For some reason, King Manoel was unhappy with the captain, even though Magellan had faithfully served Portugal for most of his life.

To gain favor with King Manoel, Magellan joined the Portuguese army in 1513. The army was fighting a war in Morocco. Although he was brave, Magellan probably should have stayed a sailor. He was seriously wounded in the leg at the Battle of Azamor. As a result, he walked with a limp for the rest of his life.

In 1515, Magellan returned to Lisbon and met with King Manoel. The sailor made three requests. First, he asked for an increase in his **pension**, a salary he received from the king. Manoel refused. Next, he asked to be assigned a mission that would allow him to regain the king's respect. Again, Manoel refused. Finally, Magellan asked if he could be allowed to serve another monarch. "Do as you please," Manoel replied testily. When Magellan bowed forward to kiss the king's ring–a sign of respect and loyalty–Manoel pulled his hand away.

After 10 years of fighting for Portugal, Magellan had been totally rejected by the king. He left Lisbon and moved to the coastal city of Oporto. There he wondered what he should do next.

Soon Magellan's imagination was tantalized by a letter that he received from his old friend Francisco Serrão. Serrão and Magellan had parted in 1511, after the capture of Malacca. When Magellan returned to Portugal, Afonso de Albuquerque had sent Serrão to find the Spice Islands. When Serrão reached the islands, his boat was wrecked. He was rescued by some natives and taken to the island of Ternate. Serrão liked the island and decided to remain. He became an adviser to the local ruler, and within a few years he had gained power and wealth. In his letter to Magellan, he wrote, "I have found a New World, richer, greater and more beautiful than that of Vasco da Gama. . . . I beg you to join me here, that you may sample for yourself the delights which surround me."

This idea tempted Magellan. Another idea took hold of him at the same time: perhaps he could sail west to the Spice Islands, instead of east through Portuguese waters. If he could find a westward route to the Indies, through the newly discovered Americas, he would succeed where Columbus had failed.

The Americas separated the Atlantic and Pacific Oceans. A sea passage between the two oceans would give the Spanish the direct route to the Indies that they desired. Magellan became obsessed with the idea of finding that passage. He returned to the Casa da India, where he had once organized sailing expeditions, and looked over old reports and maps.

Magellan soon had a plan, but he needed ships and men. There was no point in asking King Manoel. Portugal controlled the eastern route to the Spice Islands. It had no need for a route west. And the captain was still out of Manoel's good favor. Magellan decided that, like Christopher Columbus

25 years earlier, he would ask the king of Spain to sponsor the voyage. Magellan would tempt the king with the possibility of a western route to the Spice Islands—and the riches that route would bring.

Several other Portuguese captains had transferred their loyalty to Spain. One of them was João Serrão, whom Magellan had sailed with early in his career. Another was Juan Díaz de Solís, who had led a Spanish search for the sea route through the Americas. The Spanish believed there was a passage (they called it *el paso*) through the continent. De Solís found the Bay of Rio de Janeiro in 1515 but was killed by natives before discovering a waterway that connected the Atlantic to the Pacific.

Another navigator who had left Portugal, Diogo Barbosa, invited Magellan to join him in Seville and to serve the young Spanish king, Charles I. Diogo and his son, Duarte Barbosa, promised to use their influence at court to help Magellan. In October 1517, Magellan left Portugal for Spain. He stayed with the Barbosas. A few months later, Magellan married his friend's daughter, Beatriz Barbosa.

Shortly after his wedding, Magellan was invited to the court of King Charles. The sailor outlined his plan to reach the Indies, and he offered his services

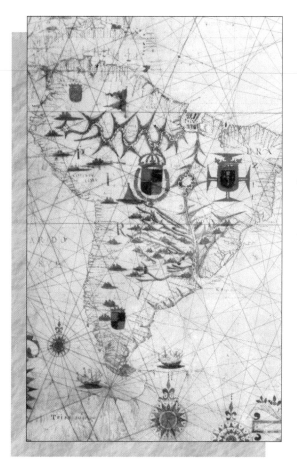

Magellan was sure that he could find a route to the East Indies by sailing west. He would succeed where Christopher Columbus had failed by finding a passage through the Americas. The ships pictured at the bottom of this 16th-century Portuguese map show where the sailor eventually would find his route.

to Spain. Charles was enthusiastic about the plan. On March 22, 1518, the king and Magellan signed a contract. The king would provide five ships and whatever funds were required to mount the expedition. He would receive four-fifths of the profits, and Magellan would get one-fifth. Magellan was named captain-general, or commander, of the expedition.

The expedition was troubled from the start. King Manoel had learned about Magellan's plans and

King Charles I was the son of King Ferdinand and Queen Isabella, the Spanish rulers who had sponsored Christopher Columbus's voyage of discovery. Magellan was pleased when the young Spanish king agreed to support his own voyage to the west.

had sent spies to disrupt the voyage. Manoel knew that if Spain found a route to the Indies, Portugal's profits and power would decline.

Another problem was that Spanish noblemen in King Charles's court were jealous of the Portuguese captain. Several experienced Spaniards had wished to lead the mission. Disappointed, they tried to sabotage the captain-general's plans. They protested that he was hiring too many Portuguese seamen who might prove disloyal to Spain.

The five ships that Magellan was given were small, old, and in need of repairs. For over a year, Magellan gathered his crew, purchased supplies, and outfitted the ships. By August 1519, Magellan was finally ready to leave Spain. He would lead the mission from his flagship, the *Trinidad*. His friend João Serrão would command the *Santiago*. The largest ship of the fleet, the *San Antonio*, was commanded by a Spanish captain named Juan de Cartagena. The *San Antonio* was loaded with food that could be shared by all the ships during the long trip. The other two ships, the *Concepción* and the *Victoria*, were also commanded by Spaniards.

Magellan was worried about the jealous Spanish captains. But the final crew of about 275 men included a number of men he knew would be loyal. These included Magellan's servant Henrique, his wife's brother Duarte Barbosa, and his cousin Alvaro de Mesquita. Another member of the crew was Antonio Pigafetta, a nobleman from Venice who told the captain that he wanted to see the wonders of the world and "the very great and awful things of the ocean."

The small fleet sailed from Seville to Sanlúcar de Barrameda on August 10, 1519. There, they loaded additional food, water, and supplies. On September 20, Magellan ordered his ships on a southern course into the Atlantic Ocean. The voyage had begun.

Seeking
El Paso

This 16th-century illustration shows some of the strange creatures that Magellan and his men expected to find on their voyage. The sailors did, in fact, encounter many strange animals as the ships traveled along the coast of South America.

5

Portugal's King Manoel had tried to disrupt Magellan's expedition when it was in port. Now Magellan was afraid the king would send Portuguese warships to harass him at sea. He believed the Portuguese would expect him to immediately sail west across the Atlantic to South America, where he would look for *el paso*, the passage through the continent. Magellan decided instead to sail south along the coast of Africa, then cut across the ocean to South America. This, he hoped, would throw off any Portuguese pursuers.

However, this route lengthened the voyage to the New World. It also brought the fleet into extremely bad weather. In November, after the ships had crossed the equator, all of the captains met on the *Trinidad.* Juan de Cartagena, captain of the *San Antonio*, demanded that the fleet's course be changed. Cartagena said he would no longer follow Magellan south. When Magellan heard this, he arrested Cartagena and imprisoned him on the *San Antonio*. This quick action stopped talk of **mutiny** (an uprising at sea) among the Spanish captains—at least for a while.

On December 13, the five caravels sailed into Rio de Janeiro Bay, on the coast of South America. Magellan's men spent two weeks there. The local Indians called this region Verzin.

While the ships were docked at Rio de Janeiro, the new captain of the *San Antonio*, Antonio de Coca, released Cartagena. Then the two Spaniards tried to stir up a revolt against Magellan. Once again, the Portuguese captain-general put down the mutinous soldiers. This time, he jailed both of the troublemakers. Magellan's cousin, Alvaro de Mesquita, was placed in command of the *San Antonio*.

The fleet remained in the warm bay until the day after Christmas. On December 26, 1519, Magellan directed his ships south to begin searching for *el paso*. As they sailed down the coast of South America, Magellan watched for waterways. Each time they passed a bay or the mouth of a river, he sent a small boat to investigate. But every one turned out to be a dead end.

As Magellan's men rested in Rio de Janeiro Bay, they traded with the Guaraní Indians who lived along the shore. The natives would trade five chickens for a fish hook, and baskets of fish for a metal bell. Both sides thought they were getting bargains!

Over the next few months, the expedition continued south into waters where no European had ever sailed. The men soon missed sunny Rio de Janeiro as the weather turned colder. Although Magellan did not know it, his route was bringing him close to frozen Antarctica. The ships' sails became tattered from sleet and high winds. The sailors' clothes and beards were caked with ice. They were exhausted from constantly battling the rough water and the winter storms.

On March 31, 1520, the small fleet entered a

narrow harbor. There, the captain-general decided to stop battling the weather and rest his men. The sheltered harbor would be a good place to stay for the rest of the winter. When the weather improved, the search for *el paso* could continue. Magellan told his men to build huts on the shore and begin looking for food. He called the place Port San Julián.

Unfortunately, Juan de Cartagena was not done stirring up trouble. He plotted with the captains of the *Victoria* and the *Concepción*, Luis de Mendoza and Gaspar de Quesada. The navigator of the *Concepción*, Juan Sebastián de Elcano, was also part of the plot. The night after the landing at Port San Julián, the rebellious officers silently led a party of men to the *San Antonio*. In the darkness, they captured Captain Mesquita while he slept and took control of the ship. On the morning of April 2, Magellan found that the Spanish captains controlled three of his ships. Only João Serrão, in the *Santiago*, remained loyal.

When Magellan's fleet landed at Port San Julián, the ships had been at sea for more than six months This was a very long voyage for the time. (Christopher Columbus's first voyage had taken only about five weeks.)

The rebels sent a message to Magellan, telling him that they would return the ships to his control if he agreed to their conditions. However, the captain-general had other plans. As a trick, he sent several men to the *Victoria* with a letter for Mendoza. At the same time another boat, hidden by fog, quietly left the *Trinidad* for the *Victoria*. On board were Duarte Barbosa and 15 good fighters loyal to Magellan.

Reportedly, Mendoza laughed scornfully when read the captain-general's message. It was his last laugh—the messenger stabbed him in the throat while the others overpowered Mendoza's guards. At the same moment, Barbosa and his sailors emerged from the fog. He led his sailors onto the deck and quickly seized control of the *Victoria*.

When the crew of the *San Antonio* saw that Magellan now commanded three ships, they ignored Quesada's commands and left their posts. Unmanned, the ship drifted closer to the *Trinidad*, and Magellan's men were able to capture the *San Antonio* without bloodshed. Now Magellan had four ships on his side. Outnumbered, Cartagena had no choice but to surrender.

Magellan was strict with the men who had rebelled. The captain-general ordered Quesada to be executed, and Cartagena, Elcano, and 45 other rebels were chained and sentenced to hard labor. Alvaro de Mesquita was restored as captain of the *San Antonio*, and he was put in charge of the prisoners. Mesquita was angry and embarrassed at having been taken by surprise. He worked the rebellious men hard. The captives were given the difficult job of pulling the heavy wooden ships onto the shore. Then they smeared the **hulls** with hot tar to keep them from leaking.

After the mutiny ended, another problem arose in Port San Julián. Magellan learned that the Portuguese spies that King Manoel had sent to sabotage his mission had succeeded. The supplies he had ordered had not all been delivered, because the spies had falsified reports. As a result, the fleet did not have enough food. Fortunately, the area was full of wildlife. Magellan's men hunted ducks, penguins, and other animals for food.

As the months passed, Magellan grew impatient. His goal was to find *el paso*. The captain-general began to think about moving the fleet south. However, he didn't realize that the harsh winter weather would become worse farther down the coast. In mid-June, Magellan sent the *Santiago* to check on

Ferdinand Magellan was a strong and determined leader. He quickly put down the attempted mutiny of the Spanish captains, and dealt harshly with the mutineers.

conditions to the south.

As soon as the *Santiago* left Port San Julián, João Serrão's ship ran into terrible storms. After 16 days, he spotted the mouth of a river, and he turned in to escape the pounding ocean. He named the river Rio de Santa Cruz. After a week, he headed back out to sea. This time, however, his boat was wrecked. Serrão and his crew survived, but had to wait at the river for a few weeks until help arrived.

At around the time the *Santiago* left Port San Julián, natives visited Magellan's campsite there for the first time. The Indians were friendly at first, but became hostile when Magellan's men tried to capture one. After the wreck of the *Santiago*, the captain-general decided to move the entire fleet south to Santa Cruz to avoid the angry Indians.

When the fleet left Port San Julián, Cartagena and another of the mutineers were left behind. They were given food, a gun, and ammunition. No one knows what became of the rebellious Spanish captain and the other mutineer. Juan Sebastián de Elcano and the other navigator who had been involved in the mutiny, Estevão Gomes, were not left behind. Their sailing skills were too important to the success of Magellan's mission.

On October 18, 1520, the fleet, now down to four ships, left Santa Cruz to continue the search for *el paso*. As they explored a large bay, a sudden storm hit. The *San Antonio* and the *Concepción* were separated from the *Trinidad* and the *Victoria* in the gale.

After two days, Magellan feared that the other two ships had been sunk. He prepared to leave the bay. Just then, lookouts saw the *San Antonio* and *Concepción*. "We saw the two ships approaching under full sail and flying their banners, coming toward us," Pigafetta later wrote in his book. "When near us,

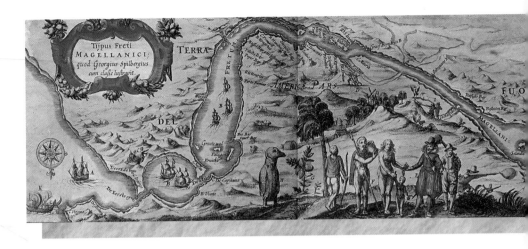

*This map from a Dutch book shows sailors meeting
Indians, and strange creatures, at the Strait of Magellan.*

they suddenly discharged their [cannons], at which
we very joyously greeted them in the same way."

Magellan soon learned that the storm had blown
the other two ships close to a rocky cliff. Trying to
avoid being wrecked, the ships had sailed into a
small waterway. At first they thought it was a creek,
but soon they discovered it was a narrow channel.
The *San Antonio* and *Concepción* followed the channel for a while. When Alvaro de Mesquita tasted the
water, it was salty. This meant that the ships were
not following a freshwater stream inland, as they
had so many times before. *El paso* had been found.

Passage to the East

6

he passage through the Americas had been found on November 1, 1520. This date is a Christian festival called the Feast of All Saints. Because of this, Magellan, a religious man, named the passage the Strait of All Saints. (A **strait** is a narrow sea passage that connects two large bodies of water.) Many years later, mapmakers would rename this passage the Strait of Magellan in his honor.

Although *el paso* had finally been discovered, sailing through it would not be easy. The 334-mile strait was narrow, rocky, and twisting. It was shallow in places and uncharted. Magellan had to be extremely cautious.

Some of the sailors, and even the officers, wanted to turn back to Spain. Now that the passage had been found, they could return and explore it another time. Magellan, however, was committed. He had a plan, and he wanted to see it through.

It took all of November for Magellan's ships to sail through the strait. By that time, his fleet had been reduced to three ships. Magellan awoke one morning to find the *San Antonio* gone. Thinking the ship had gotten lost, he spent weeks searching the area. It turned out that a group of Spaniards, led by the mutinous pilot Estevão Gomes, had overpowered Alvaro de Mesquita, the captain of the *San Antonio*. They imprisoned Mesquita and turned the ship back to Spain. This was a terrible loss, because the *San Antonio* carried most of the fleet's **provisions**.

On November 28, 1520, the *Trinidad*, the *Concepción*, and the *Victoria* emerged from the rough waters of the strait into a calm sea. This was the body of water that Vasco Núñez de Balboa had discovered in 1513 and called the South Sea. Because the ocean water was tranquil when compared with the choppy, dangerous strait, Magellan called it the *Mar Pacífico*, or peaceful sea. (This led to the name it is known by today, the Pacific Ocean.)

When they exited the strait, Magellan and his men believed that their voyage was nearing its end. The Spice Islands couldn't be far, they thought. Unfortunately, no one realized that the Pacific Ocean is an enormous body of water. The Spice Islands were still thousands of miles away.

Magellan's three-caravel fleet sailed north along the coast of South America until mid-December. Then it headed west across the Pacific. It would be 98 days before the sailors saw inhabited land again.

Before they had left South America, Magellan had ordered his men to store as much food as they could in the holds of the three ships. But as the journey stretched on, the food began to rot and the drinking water stagnated. And because the ships did not carry fresh fruit or vegetables, the sailors' diets did not include vitamin C. Lack of this vitamin causes a disease called scurvy. Soon the

In his book on the voyage, Antonio Pigafetta explained how the sailors coped without food. "We ate old biscuit reduced to powder and full of grubs, and drank water that was yellow and stinking," Pigafetta wrote. "We ate the oxhides from under the yardarms, also the sawdust of wood, and rats."

men's arms and legs ached, and their gums became painfully swollen.

Then some of the sailors began to die. Pigafetta reported that 19 men were killed by disease and starvation. Many others were too weak to work.

On January 24, 1521, the fleet stopped at a small, deserted island. There, they refilled their supply of fresh water. In February, the caravels crossed the equator for the second time. Finally, on March 5, three islands were sighted.

Magellan gave orders for the fleet to anchor off what today is the island of Guam. Natives from the island immediately rowed their canoes out to the three ships. They were friendly, but they helped themselves to everything that they could carry: rope, metal tools, and even a small boat on the *Trinidad.* The captain-general sent his men after the natives, ordering them to reclaim the fleet's supplies and get food so the voyage could continue. The men brought back the equipment, along with bananas, fish, coconuts, and sweet potatoes. When Magellan left, he named the island the Isle of Thieves.

The surviving sailors were strengthened by this food. They were also heartened when, 10 days later, Magellan's lookouts spotted a group of many green

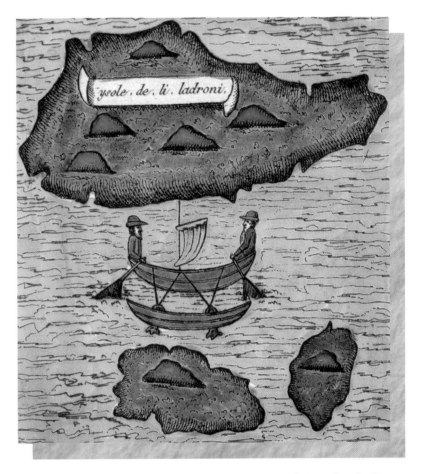

ysole. de. li. ladroni.

This colorful picture from Antonio Pigafetta's book shows two sailors trying out a native outrigger canoe at Guam. After encountering the Indians, Magellan named the island Las Islas de Ladrones—the Isle of Thieves.

islands rising out of the sea. They had discovered a chain of 7,000 islands: the Philippines. The 13,000-mile voyage across the Pacific had taken 108 days. "Nevermore will any man undertake to make such a voyage," Pigafetta later wrote.

The Philippines are located in the South China Sea. This region was known to many of the European sailors. João Serrão urged Magellan to make a brief stop and load the ships with food and supplies. He was sure that they could easily find the Spice Islands. Serrão argued that Magellan could pick up a cargo in the Spice Islands, then return to Spain by the well-known Portuguese route around Africa. The captain-general would gain fame for finding *el paso*, and riches by selling the spices.

Serrão could not persuade Magellan. The stubborn captain-general had claimed the islands for Spain, and he insisted on exploring them. As usual, the determined sailor got his way.

Converting heathens to Christianity was an important goal of Spanish explorers and conquistadors. They felt that it was their duty to bring the Christian religion to heathens in the new lands they found.

When the fleet reached the island of Limasawa, Magellan's servant Henrique could understand the natives' language. He translated conversations between the Europeans and Colambu, the *rajah*, or ruler, of the island. Colambu offered to take Magellan to the overlord of all the islands, Rajah

Humabon. Colambu led Magellan's fleet to Cebu, the capital of the islands. There, the Spaniards converted the natives to Christianity.

On one island, Mactan, the rajah refused to convert. Mactan's rajah, Lapulapu, and his people were the enemies of Rajah Humabon. The natives asked Magellan to punish Lapulapu. Although Serrão and his friends urged the captain-general not to get involved, Magellan agreed to Humabon's request.

On April 27, 1521, Ferdinand Magellan led a troop of about 60 men to Mactan. With the *Trinidad*, *Concepción*, and *Victoria* anchored offshore, they rowed to the beach to teach the natives a lesson.

The attack was a disaster. Magellan's men had to wade ashore wearing heavy armor. When the battle began, they were quickly overwhelmed by thousands of natives. As their comrades began to fall, many of the Spanish soldiers fled the battlefield.

Bravely, Magellan remained on the beach, covering their retreat. Only a handful of soldiers stood with him. One of them was Pigafetta. Another was the servant Henrique. João Serrão and Duarte Barbosa, Magellan's closest friends, were watching the fight from their ships. Yet for some reason, they did not send reinforcements to help the captain-general.

Leading an assault on the island of Mactan on April 27, 1521, Ferdinand Magellan was overwhelmed by the natives and killed.

Magellan courageously battled the natives for about an hour. Then he was wounded in the arm and leg. He fell face down in the shallow water. At Magellan's death, the remaining soldiers scrambled to escape the battlefield. The brave captain-general's body was never recovered.

After the death of Ferdinand Magellan, the expedition became a disaster. The three ships returned to Cebu. The Portuguese did not realize that the natives wanted to capture the three caravels. Rajah

Humabon invited Serrão, Barbosa, and the other officers to a feast on shore. When they arrived, Humabon's warriors slaughtered the European leaders.

At this point, only about 120 men remained of the original crew of 275. This was not enough to sail the three ships. The survivors divided the supplies between the *Victoria* and the *Trinidad* and sank the leaky *Concepción*. Then the two ships headed for the Spice Islands. On the way, however, they attacked several ships and captured their cargoes. If Magellan had been alive, these acts of ***piracy*** would never have been allowed.

On November 6, 1521, the ships finally sighted the Spice Islands. It had been 820 days since they had left Seville. The fleet had sailed over 28,000 miles. They landed in Tidore to find that Francisco Serrão was dead. However, the sultan gave them a valuable cargo of spices to take back to Spain.

While they were in port, the *Trinidad* sprang a leak. It would take a long time to repair. The sailors were anxious to get home. They were also undecided about what to do next. Some wanted to sail around Africa and return to Spain. This way was much shorter, and it was also well known, but the

Spanish ship would be traveling in unfriendly territory controlled by Spain's enemy, Portugal.

Others wanted to return to Spain the way they had come, through the Strait of Magellan. This way would be safe from Portuguese warships, but it would mean a repeat of the long journey that had brought the sailors this far.

The men decided to take the ships in separate directions. A group of 54 men repaired the *Trinidad* and tried to retrace their route through the strait. They never made it. Storms forced the ship to return to the Spice Islands, where it was captured by the Portuguese. The survivors were imprisoned for many years. A few eventually reached Spain.

Juan Sebastián de Elcano, who was now the senior officer on the *Victoria*, took the remaining 47 men around the Cape of Good Hope. The *Victoria*'s trip was not easy. Elcano had to avoid coastal ports, as these were controlled by the Portuguese. The food rotted, as it had on the Pacific voyage, and many men died. And a rough storm in the Cape of Good Hope destroyed one of the *Victoria*'s three masts. This slowed her progress even more.

Finally, on September 6, 1522, the caravel reached Sanlúcar de Barrameda. Of the original

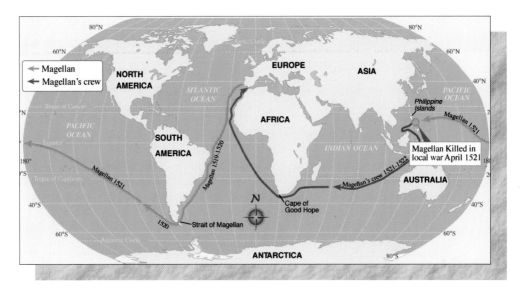

This map shows the route that Magellan's ships took in circling the world from 1519 to 1522.

crew, only 18 had survived the journey. The Spaniards praised Elcano as a national hero. They gave him most of the credit for the voyage, overlooking his role in the mutiny against Magellan.

Magellan's accomplishments were not recognized until years later. Today he is regarded as a brave explorer and a resourceful commander. His daring navigation and his discovery of the strait inspired many later mariners. Ferdinand Magellan's voyage was the culmination of an incredible century of discovery that had started with Prince Henry the Navigator in 1419. It would usher in another period of exploration–the Great Age of Discovery.

Chronology

1419 Prince Henry the Navigator launches the era of Portuguese exploration.

1480 Fernão de Magalhães (Ferdinand Magellan) born in northern Portugal.

1487 Bartolomeu Dias rounds the Cape of Good Hope.

1492 Christopher Columbus discovers what he believes is a westerly route to the East Indies, which later turns out to be the New World; Magellan becomes a royal page in Lisbon.

1496 Magellan promoted to squire; takes clerk position in the Casa da India.

1498 Vasco da Gama reaches India, establishing a Portuguese trade route to the East Indies.

1505 Magellan sails with the armada of Francisco de Almeida to Africa and India.

1507 Magellan sails with Nuno Pereira.

1509 Magellan is badly wounded in an attack on the Arab fleet; takes part in failed assault on city of Malacca; promoted to captain.

1510 Magellan decides to return to Portugal, but is shipwrecked and loses his fortune; decides to continue fighting in the Indian Ocean.

1511 Participates in capture of Malacca; returns to Lisbon to find he is out of favor with King Manoel.

1513 Joins Portuguese military; wounded in Battle of Azamor; court-martialed, but cleared of wrongdoing.

1515   Dismissed from service by King Manoel

1517   Leaves Portugal for Spain.

1518   Marries Beatriz Barbosa; outlines plans for westward expedition to the Indies for King Charles of Spain.

1519   Magellan's fleet of five ships set sail in August.

1520   Magellan discovers the strait that bears his name; his fleet, now down to three ships, enters the Pacific Ocean in November.

1521   Magellan sails across the Pacific and discovers the Philippine Islands; killed April 27 in assault on the island of Mactan; King Manoel of Portugal dies in December.

1522   The *Victoria*, commanded by Juan Sebastián de Elcano and manned by 18 men, arrives in Spain, concluding the first circumnavigation of the world.

Glossary

armada–a fleet of warships.

astronomy–the study of objects and matter that are outside the earth's atmosphere, such as the stars and planets. Because sailors used the stars to guide their journeys, an understanding of astronomy was important for navigation.

caravan–a company of travelers on a journey through desert or hostile regions. People traveled in caravans to protect themselves from bandits and brigands.

caravel–a sturdy sailing ship developed by the Portuguese in the 15th century. Caravels had broad hulls, a high and narrow deck at the at the back, and three masts.

circumnavigate–to sail around the world.

coat of arms–a symbolic emblem that depicts a person's heritage or accomplishments.

court-martial–the trial of a person in the military.

dhow–an Arab sailing ship with triangular sails (this is called "lateen rigging").

equator–an imaginary east-west line that divides the earth into two equal parts, the Northern and Southern hemispheres.

geography–the study of the earth's form, and its division into land and sea areas.

hull–the main frame and body of a ship, not including the masts, sails, or rigging.

mutiny–a revolt by a ship's crew against discipline or against a commanding officer.

navigation–the science of directing the course of a seagoing vessel, and of determining its position.

nobility–the ruling class of a country or state, or a group of people holding special privileges.

page–a young person who serves as an attendant for a person of noble rank. The duties of a page included delivering messages and serving as guides.

peninsula–a land area surrounded on three sides by water.

pension–a fixed amount of money that is paid regularly to a person. A country's ruler or government may grant a pension to someone who deserves a reward for service.

piracy–an act of robbery on the high seas.

provisions–a stock of food and water.

rajah–a noble title used by an Indian or Malay ruler.

scurvy–a disease caused by lack of vitamin C, which was common on long sea voyages. Its signs include spongy gums and loose teeth, soreness in the arm and leg joints, and bleeding into the skin and mucous membranes.

spices–any of various aromatic vegetable products, such as pepper or nutmeg, used to season or flavor foods. In the 15th and 16th centuries, spices were rare and highly valued by the people of Europe.

squire–the armor bearer of a knight–a rank above page.

strait–a relatively narrow passageway that connects two large bodies of water.

sultan–a title referring to the king or ruler of a Muslim city or country.

Further Reading

Columbus, Christopher, and Antonio Pigafetta. *To America and Around the World: The Logs of Christopher Columbus and of Ferdinand Magellan.* Boston: Branden Publishing, 1991.

Fritz, Jean. *Around the World in a Hundred Years: From Henry the Navigator to Magellan.* Illustrated by Anthony Bacon Venti. New York: Putnam Publishing Group, 1994.

Guillemard, Francis H. *Life of Ferdinand Magellan and the First Circumnavigation of the Globe.* New York: AMS Press, 1990.

Hynson, Colin. *Magellan and the Exploration of South America.* Hauppauge, NY: Barrons Juveniles, 1998.

Jacobs, William Jay. *Magellan : Voyager with a Dream.* Danbury, CT: Franklin Watts, 1994.

MacDonald, Fiona. *Magellan : A Voyage Around the World.* Danbury, CT: Franklin Watts, 1998.

Mason, Antony, and Keith Lye. *The Children's Atlas of Exploration: Follow in the Footsteps of the Great Explorers.* Brookfield, CT: Millbrook Press, 1993.

Noonan, Jon. *Ferdinand Magellan.* New York: Crestwood House, 1993.

Stefoff, Rebecca. *Ferdinand Magellan and the Discovery of the World Ocean.* New York: Chelsea House Publishers, 1990.

———. *Vasco da Gama and the Portuguese Explorers.* New York: Chelsea House Publishers, 1993.

Picture Credits

JIM GALLAGHER is the author of more than 10 books for young adults, including biographies of Vasco da Gama and Hernando de Soto in the Chelsea House series EXPLORERS OF NEW WORLDS. A former newspaper editor and publisher, he lives near Philadelphia.